A Cultured Girl

A Collection of Poems and Short Stories

Written and Illustrated by Terri Mash

Contributions by Mary Mash Whalen and Dee Mash Johnson

Monday Creek Publishing
Ohio USA

Copyright © Terri Mash 2019
All poems and artwork by Terri Mash, except where noted.
Contributing Editor Dee Mash Johnson

Printed in the United States of America

Monday Creek Publishing, Ohio, USA
mondaycreekpublishing.com

To Mom and Dad

Jesse Mary Ronald Diana Donald Terri

CONTENTS

Morning Glory 1

First Day of School 2

The Secret 4

Where I'm From 6

Bath Time 8

Donald's Half 11

Mary 13

The Person Inside 14

Laundry Day 16

No Laughing Allowed 18

Grandma's Little Cottage 20

Good Morning Glory 22

Mr. Gibson 24

Missing You 26

Bluebird 28

Appalachian Child 30

Contessa 33

Twilight at Lake Snowden 35

Blessings of Spring 36

Mother Nature 38

The Bug Band Camping Song 40

My Coffee 43

Wannabe 44

A Cultured Girl 46

Housekeeper's Blues 48

Her College Education 50

Friendship 52

Whisper My Name 55

Emma Rose 57

Amen 58

Put the Phone Down 60

Unconditional Love 62

Sandy 63

The Master 64

Blondie 68

My Gray Speckled Horse 71

A Healing Time 73

All Things Good 76

A Cowboy's Wisdom 79

A Contented Life 80

Picnic with a Squirrel 85

Miracles Happen 86

Fall For Nita 88

Reflection 90

The Woman 92

My Song 94

A Cultured Girl's World 98

The Child Inside 100

Winter's Edge 102

A Round House 104

When Kindness Goes Away 111

In Loving Memory of Mattie Mash on Mother's Day 113

Preface

This is my first book and bears the title *A Cultured Girl*. It is a great opportunity to pay tribute to my family. It introduces you, the reader, to special people in my life. First, my Grandmother who endured many hardships in her life but taught all six of us many valuable lessons. It is from her that I learned to appreciate nature and to spark my imagination. Also, my brothers and sisters, who still stay close and have brought me great joy. You will meet my life partner and companion John "Jock" Adams.

My family's musical background influenced my writing. I have put many of my poems to music and enjoy "front porch picking." In the process of writing this book, I discovered it is sometimes stressful and difficult to reimagine the past. This only made me more determined to complete what I had started. I hope it kindles fond memories of days gone by and makes you smile.

Acknowledgements

I want to thank my parents for giving me zany brothers and sisters to grow up and grow old with. My brother, Ron, for opening my mind and sharing his steadfast positive "can do" attitude. My sisters for their contributions. My sister, Dee, for her endless advice and editing. Also, I want to thank my other half, Jock; his critiques, for eating bologna sandwiches and potpies while I wrote and drew my illustrations. He was by my side through this whole project. I also give thanks to God for making all things possible.

MORNING GLORY

Mornings would find her pulling the hand-stitched quilt up over her feather-bed. Then she would put on her handmade shawl and step out on the back porch of her two-room cottage ready to start her day.

She followed the path up to her garden where she worked pulling weeds and tended the young plants. She liked the way the dirt felt, moist with morning dew, in her hands. Next, she goes to the trellis to check her favorite flower, the morning glory. She picks one and rubs the soft flower against her face, weathered from time and hard work. She puts the flower under her nose, closes her eyes and enjoys its sweet scent.

She walks up the path to the big house where her daughter and son-in-law live with their children, her grandchildren, six in all. She slips quietly in the back door, washes her hands and pulls skillets and pans from the cupboards.

She works quietly. The bacon was frying as she cracked the eggs and got butter and bread out for toast. She brewed a pot of coffee. She heard the children stirring upstairs and knew she only had minutes before they came rumbling down the stairs to start their day. This was her favorite part of the day.

FIRST DAY OF SCHOOL

I was so excited for my first day of school. I was going to get to run down the long driveway with my brothers and sisters and catch the bus.

We each had a new yellow-lined tablet that had an Indian head on the cover. I had a big fat pencil to learn to print my ABC's. Mom bought me a new blue dress that had trim around the short sleeves and around the full part above the hem. The skirt flowed out when I twirled. It had a big white collar with a bow under my neck. I wore white socks with saddle shoes.

Mom took us all outside and she took our "first day of school" picture. When we heard the bus coming down the road, we all made our way down the driveway to the bus stop. I remember the sound the doors made as they swung open. I was very small for my age, the step looked so high and big, and I was scared.

At that moment, I felt my oldest brother Jesse put his hands under my arms and lift me upon the bus. The driver's name was Mr. Stage and he smiled when I climbed on the seat with my feet sticking straight out. He closed the door and I began a new journey.

Back row: Ronald, Jesse, Mary
Front row: Terri, Donald, Diana

THE SECRET

I can still remember vividly the first grade and my wonderful teacher, Mrs. Carpenter. She was caring, patient and had a very gentle voice. She had a way of making each student feel special. Mrs. Carpenter taught us to read and write which opened an exciting world to me.

It was early November, chilly, and winter was on its way. One day at school we noticed a brown box sitting on her desk. The class wondered what it was but never asked, and she never revealed its contents. At the end of the day when we were leaving the classroom to catch the bus, she tapped me on the shoulder and quietly asked me to stay a few minutes. The other children put on their wraps and left the room. She had me stand up and brought the mysterious brown box to me and began to open it. It contained the most beautiful little royal blue coat I had ever seen. It had a velvet collar and three large buttons down the front. I tried it on and it fit perfectly.

I can't put into words the happiness I felt. Mrs. Carpenter told me this would be our secret. She put it back in the box with a note to my mom and I went home. Mom opened the box, put the coat on me, then read the note. She had tears in her eyes. I loved the coat and my first grade teacher. I don't know if she ever realized how much joy she brought to this little girl with that secret.

my little blue coat

WHERE I'M FROM
by Diana Lynn Mash Johnson

I'm from no indoor plumbing
From an old coal stove
That we would circle around for warmth
From strong coffee to cigarette smoke as
Thick and dense as pea soup

From playing kick-the-can, black and white T.V.
The middle sibling of Mary and Terri
(the rhyming sisters)

I'm from my Dad with an eighth-grade education
Who loved to read
From my Mom who we would circle around
To absorb her warmth
Depend on her for strength

I'm from dreams to rise above my roots
To a family that grounds me
From seeing the stars
But not fully reaching them

BATH TIME

We used to take baths on Sunday nights in a #2 round washtub with water retrieved earlier in the day from a spring out back. Grandma and us children would help with this chore.

Mom heated the water on the coal stove in the dining room. There were six children to bathe and dry, so this was a very laborious task. She did it as quickly and as efficiently as she could, scrubbing us roughly, drying us, then putting on our pajamas. She added more hot water, then time for the next one. I was the youngest, so the water was usually just lukewarm by the time I got my bath. There was no time to linger or play in the tub. So it is no wonder that one thing I love to do now is take long hot soaks in the tub. I will never forget those days and Sunday night baths in the #2 tub.

DONALD'S HALF

He had a crop of tousled blonde hair
Seven years old, an impish little grin
The trouble he got into, well, let me just begin
My dad was a wheeler-dealer in those days
Fix it up, paint it red, put it out to sell
Money to be made to feed six kids
He couldn't let it fail
He had an old blue 1954 truck sitting in the yard
Donald loved it, dad said, "Son it's half yours."
He didn't realize the gravity of those words
And how they would affect a seven year old boy
Dad went to the house to have his coffee
Left my brother out to play
Oh, what a mistake that was on this warm summer day
He found my brother covered in red paint
The truck was smeared from bumper to the door
He couldn't believe what he was seeing
He let out quite a roar
Dad's face was red with anger that day
Through the years the story brought us quite a laugh
His innocent little blonde haired boy
Said, "Dad, I only painted my half."

LADYBUG

MARY

She had shiny blonde hair
Was fair of face
Always pleasant with a
Gentle grace

She ironed for hours
Cleaned house and took care of us
Until Mom got home

She had a cat named Ladybug
But never had a bicycle
She was the heart of the family

Mary

THE PERSON INSIDE

She guards her heart
With eyes of steel
Stands her ground
With a stubborn will

She protects what is hers
She takes control
Grasping tight
She won't let go

What makes her so strong
I would like to know
The person inside
Who won't let go

Dee

"It was nice growing up with someone like you –
someone to lean on, someone to count on…
someone to tell on."

LAUNDRY DAY

Mom used to do laundry in an old Wringer washer that was on the back porch. This took hours. She would take the wet flat clothes to the clothesline, then holler for me. I remember taking the bag full of clothespins and handing them to her one by one as she hung up clothes, sheets, and towels.

Flapping in the warm breeze, it didn't take long for it all to dry. We would then go get everything off the line. The chore wasn't too bad in the summertime, but winter, however, it was something I always dreaded. I remember how mom's hands would almost be blue by the time we were done. Being so young, I didn't understand how hard this chore was for her, and I would whine and complain because she had me come out and hand her clothespins. It took years and maturity for me to understand how hard she worked and all the sacrifices she made for us. I think about it now as I throw the clothes in the washer and go back and toss them in the dryer.

NO LAUGHING ALLOWED

Three to a bed
Underneath an itchy gray blanket
Too cold or too warm
Curlers in our hair

Chairs around a coal stove
Grandma fixing breakfast
Off to school

Supper at the big table
No laughing allowed
We laughed anyway

Mary the Rose

Terri
the dreamer

Diana
the realist

Terri
the
Dreamer

Dee the
Realist

the sisters three

The sisters three.

Tranquil Beauty
Family Love
I am Rich

GRANDMA'S LITTLE COTTAGE

Through the vines and the brambles
Past the oak tree near the pines
Sits grandma's little cottage
Still vivid in my mind

The aroma of homemade apple butter
The big, soft feather bed
Snapping beans from the garden
She kept our family fed

She took us berry picking
We dug roots, made sassafras tea
Each day was an adventure
She meant the world to me

I wish I could go back in time
And see her twinkling eyes
Listen to her wisdom
Of yesterday's gone by

21

GOOD MORNING GLORY

Good morning, glory
With your trumpet so blue
Winding through the trellis
Your vines fresh with dew
A quiet morning beauty
Makes my heart smile
A tender blessed moment
That stays for awhile

MR. GIBSON

There's an old guitar in the parlor
My Father used to play
He called it Mr. Gibson
And it would be mine some day

He sang his songs for his family
The neighbors and a few good friends
They loved Dad and Mr. Gibson
I thought those days would never end

Years flew by and he taught me
To sing his songs and pick those strings
Me and Mr. Gibson
Could play most anything

Yes, I hit the big time
Everyone knows my name
Sold out shows on the road
But there's a price to pay for fame

My heart is with my family
My neighbors and friends
In the parlor sits Mr. Gibson
I long to see them all again

Mr. Gibson

MISSING YOU

My dreams are drifting softly
My hopes are soaring high
I know that I can touch the stars
And see you in the sky

There's your face, you're smiling now
I can almost touch your cheek
The light grows dim, you fade away
It leaves my body weak

Someday I will join you
We will rejoice in heaven's light
Today my heart is missing you
As I hold your memory tight

Mom

I am the dreamer
At the end of the line
Trying to catch up
Always running behind
Distracted by a bird
Or a rabbit or by
The shape of a cloud...

BLUEBIRD

I saw a bluebird, a pretty bluebird
Sitting in an old oak tree
And that bluebird, that pretty bluebird
Sang his song just for me

He sang be happy, be oh so happy
Don't let your life pass you by
For tomorrow is not promised
I don't want to see you cry

I have a bluebird box
In my front yard
My brother Jesse made for me
I love sitting on the front porch
Watching bluebirds in the trees

Jock and I love to spend time
On the front porch enjoying the
Breeze and watching nature
I wouldn't trade this quiet
Time for anything

Thanks, Jesse

APPALACHIAN CHILD

I've never rode on a subway or seen the liberty bell

I haven't touched the tall redwoods and probably never will

I'm just a child of Appalachia who loves the golden leaves and morning dew

The deer running through the forest; robin eggs bright and blue

I love the red sky of sunset, cherry blossoms in the spring,

the long lazy days of summer, the chill that autumn brings.

Someday I'll ride the subway, and soar high o'er the redwood tree,

When the bell tolls as my Father calls, and sets my spirit free.

"Contessa"

Dedicated to Liz

CONTESSA

Contessa was a royal cat
Who sat upon a satin pillow
Her humans scrambled all about
While Contessa stretched and felt quite mellow

They worked hard and fretted much
Bought toys and laid them at her paws
She was fed the finest gourmet foods
Yes, Contessa the royal princess cat
Really had it all

She knew she was special from the day
The smallest human picked her from the others
From an overcrowded shelter cage
She had to leave her mother

She did her best to please them
She purred and engaged them in her play
She climbed up the back of the royal couch
And napped in the sunshine rays

*If you want to enrich your life and have royalty in her your home,
please consider adopting a shelter cat.*

34

TWILIGHT AT LAKE SNOWDEN

Campfires flickering through the trees
Children's laughter upon the breeze

Peaceful reflection of the day
Life's worries melting away

Night sounds are calming
Under a silvery moon

Renewing my soul
With nature's tune

BLESSINGS OF SPRING

I like to watch the fledglings
Take flight in early Spring
I like to see the trees bud out
And hear the robin sing

I like to hear the peepers
And feel the warm evening breeze
I like to wade in creek beds
With cool water to my knees

These things make me happy
My heart feels such content
I enjoy all the blessings of Spring
It is time well spent

MOTHER NATURE

I'm amazed by the quiet flight of the butterfly,
and the buzzing of the noisy little bee
I see the beauty of Mother Nature
As she shares her gifts with me

Today she gives me sunshine,
yesterday she sent a pounding rain,
with rumbling thunder and fierce lightning,
her wrath won out again.

She rules the world her way,
I accept it with a guarded truce,
I both respect and fear her wisdom,
as she sets her power loose

My dog Sandy and I are afraid of storms, we "weather" them out together.

THE BUG BAND CAMPING SONG

Sittin' round the campfire
Tellin' stories with my friends
Roastin' weenies and makin' smores
Then the music begins

Skeeter plays the guitar
June bug plays the drum
Froggy's back on bass
As Katydid sings the songs

The crickets chirp in harmony
It echoes through the night
As fireflies flutter all around
To give it all some light

The forest is alive with music
The stars twinkle up above
Songs float upon a breeze
And fill the trees with love

Oh, the Bug Band plays nature's tunes
For all of us to hear
They start up in the springtime
And quit when winter's near

Come along and join us
You'll have a lot of fun
Listening to the Bug Band
'Til the rising of the sun

COFFEE

SOOTHES THAT MORNING MONSTER

MY COFFEE

I was feeling quite poorly
Come a Monday morn
Depleted and weary
Confused and forlorn

They rushed me to the hospital
I received intensive care
But nothing seemed to help me
The doctors felt despair
They scratched their heads in confusion
They didn't know what to do
They tried all their medicine
But I still didn't come to

There was a passerby with coffee
I jerked as I caught a whiff
The nurse saw my nose move
And put a drop upon my lip

I opened my eyes instantly
So, she gave me more
I drank a cup of coffee
Then walked out of the door

WANNABE

Look at the person inside of me
Not who I am, but who I wannabe
I am a cowgirl
Roping and riding in my dreams
I climb dangerous mountain passes
I cross swift rivers and jump flowing streams

I am a cowgirl
Riding fast, fast, fast
Hooves pounding on the ground
Through the fields of tall grass

I control my wild steed
With a confident hand
We are the finest
Throughout God's land

Reality finds me
By the gate in sorrow
I wannabe a cowgirl
Maybe tomorrow

A CULTURED GIRL

I want to soar on eagle's wings
To feel what it's like to fly
Float up over mountains
As misty clouds pass by

I want to swim broad oceans
And see creatures of the deep
Sit upon a whale's back
When it takes a mighty leap

I want to travel all the lands
Make friends throughout the world
Learn of different customs
And be a cultured girl

But now I must finish mopping the floor
Maybe wash a window or two
Because I am a housekeeper
And that is what I do

HOUSEKEEPER'S BLUES

Moppin' the floors and
Washin' the walls
I do it every day
Wish I had a red Corvette
And I would just ride away
I'd go cruisin', cruisin', cruisin' through the neighborhood

Sittin' on my front porch
Rockin' in my chair
I see the birds in the trees
Off they fly in the air
And float upon the breeze
They're cruisin', cruisin', cruisin' in the neighborhood

I bought some bait at the corner store
The fish were bitin' so I bought some more
The sun went down and the stars shone bright
The frogs are croakin' - gonna sleep good tonight
I'll be snoozin', snoozin', snoozin' in the neighborhood

I wrote this little song at work.

HER COLLEGE EDUCATION

Her job was working second shift, 4:30 p.m. until 1 a.m. at a local university. She cleaned in a multicultural building where there were student-teaching assistants and faculty offices, plus many classrooms. It was a building that taught linguistics, foreign languages and intensive English. The last half of the shift was spent emptying trash cans and washing blackboards in the classrooms. Being of very small stature she used a window washing kit to achieve this task. This made her arms ache at the end of each work night.

To help get through the monotonous humdrum of the job, she started reading the blackboards each night and found it very interesting. Also, handouts that had fallen on the floor with class assignments on them triggered her curiosity. She started to study them during her break times, absorbing the knowledge. It made her wonder what life would have been like if she had a better education. Sometimes this depressed her and made her feel sorry for herself, but as time went on this changed.

She began talking to the students, a majority of them from other countries. They told her stories and what life was like in far-away lands. It sparked an interest in her to learn new things on her own. By doing this she noticed her positivity and confidence grew and helped change her outlook on life.

Drawing, writing poems, songs, and stories had always been her hobby. But she destroyed them or hid them away thinking they were childish and foolish. This too changed with time as she gained confidence and matured in her attitude and outlook. She started to keep her stories and shared them with others. It gave her great gratification. She realized that you can learn and create on your own with determination. Life is a continuing education if you open your mind and gather knowledge from your surroundings.

My sincere thanks to all the people of Gordy Hall, Ohio University, Athens, Ohio.

FRIENDSHIP

For Katherine (Kitten) Lynn Mash

When I find a feather
When I climb the next hill
I will think of forever
And of a time that stood still

I will remember the laughter and good times
The jokes and the tears
I will cherish a friendship that will last all my years

Loves may come and go
Like ships out to sea
But a friend that lasts forever
Is what you've given me

Quiet is the forest and strong is the tree
Thank God I had a friend like you
To love and comfort me

IN MEMORY OF

KATHERINE LYNN "KITTEN" MASH

DATE OF BIRTH
November 14, 1957

DATE OF DEATH
January 7,1997

I wrote this in remembrance of my sister-in-law Kathy (Kitten who died too young) at 39 years old. She took such pleasure in the small things in life, like finding a feather. She was loyal, family oriented, and inspiring.

In the morning you will see the glory of the Lord.
Exodus 16:7

WHISPER MY NAME

A gentle breeze is blowing
A white light is glowing
As I hear Jesus whisper my name
He says, "Come with me,
I will take care of thee."
As I hear Jesus whisper my name
Don't look back at the world you left behind
There are loved ones waiting for you
Heaven's gates are just ahead
And I hear Jesus whisper my name

EMMA ROSE

Pretty blue eyes
And a button of a nose
Ten tiny fingers and
Ten tiny toes

Chubby little cheeks
And soft baby skin
She coos and wiggles
And gives a little grin

I can't imagine life without
My Emma Rose
A perfect angel from her
Head to her toes

You are safe and loved in
This ole world
I will always take care of
My baby girl

Six months old and your eyes
Have turned brown
Mommy's little princess and
Daddy's little clown

You wake up with a smile
On your face everyday
And make funny little faces
As you play

AMEN

The little girl looked pleadingly up
At the vet with tears in her eyes
She was holding her puppy in her arms
Trying hard not to cry

He had gotten away she said
And ran into a busy street
"Help him please, I love him so"
Her little face held such defeat

Her father stood quietly by
And watched the scene unfold
As he remembered a little dog
He had so many years ago

His name was Jake, a faithful friend
Yes, they were quite the pair
The vet just shook his head
As her father said a prayer

Just as he said Amen
They saw the puppy twitch
They could hardly believe their ears
When they heard the puppy yip

The vet threw up his hands in surprise
For the pup had surely been dead
"There must have been a special power
In the prayer your father said!"

McKenna Adams holding Misty Blu.

PUT THE PHONE DOWN

Put the phone down and play with me
I'm only on this earth a short while you see
I'm here to make you happy and absorb some of your pain
Put the phone down and play with me
You have the world to gain

Come out into the sunshine
Leave worries and troubles behind
Throw the ball, we'll play fetch
We will have a good time

I know you are the master
But I think you need a break
You can take me for a walk
We can romp down by the lake
Put the phone down and play with me

Put down the phone.

UNCONDITIONAL LOVE

She warms my heart with her soft brown eyes
She keeps my secrets, she tells no lies
Her love is unconditional

She's excited to see me after work each day
She brings me a toy, she wants me to play

She's there when I'm sad and lonely
She shares in my pain
My constant companion
Even though I complain

The years have rolled quickly
She's crippled and slow
Her vision is fading
But one thing I know
Her love is unconditional

I will cherish and comfort her
Until her life's very end
As she took care of me
She's my very best friend
My love for her is unconditional

The Author, Terri, and her dog.

SANDY

It was July of 2006. Jock had just retired and wanted a dog. We wanted one that was already housebroken and that would also serve as a watchdog. An advertisement in the local newspaper for an eight month old female Australian shepherd and golden retriever mix caught our attention. We decided to check her out. A young couple had just moved to Ohio from New York and were expecting a child. They needed to rehome Sandy. She was beautiful. The first thing she did was jump on Jock in excitement and lay open his arm with a big scratch. We brought her home anyway. Sandy didn't turn out to be a watchdog. She is very gentle and loving, and she doesn't know a stranger. Sandy has greatly enriched our lives.

"I would buy her a golden bed if I could."

THE MASTER

A little dog by the roadside
Shivering and alone
Dumped out by his master
Now he has no home
Days went by and no rescue
He lived in the woods alone

Two hunters found his body
Curled up under a tree
Still waiting for his master's return
That he never lived to see

Life doesn't always have happy endings
Sometimes it can be so cruel
When we get to that crossroad
Will we know what to do?

One love was forever
Always faithful, always true
The other was fleeting
What kind of master are you?

Please be a good master.

It came to me that every time I lose a dog they take a piece of my heart with them, and every new dog who comes into my life gifts me with a piece of their heart. If I live long enough all the components of my heart will be dog, and I will become as generous and loving as they are.

Anonymous

Zoey

BLONDIE

He had a special bond with a
Horse he named Blondie
She ran to greet him when his truck pulled in each day
On long cold winter nights, he rubbed her down and fed her extra hay
They rode the trails together, forged through
The fields and streams
A quiet understanding
Oh, what a beautiful thing
A man needs something in his life he can
Call his own...

When I think of Jock, the word proud comes to mind. He is so strong-willed and determined, he is one of a kind. His love for animals and the way they respond to him is amazing to watch.

MY GRAY SPECKLED HORSE

My love for her is never-ending
I really don't understand

I feel so blessed to have her
I guess it was a part of God's plan

I feel very humble and thankful
As my life runs its course

To share it with such a beautiful creature
As my gray speckled horse!

A HEALING TIME

It was late summer when I became a companion for a horse named Blondie. Before they got me, I had suffered from neglect and had been in several different homes. The Chevy truck with a stock trailer was scary to me. I wasn't sure what was happening, but past circumstances had me on edge. When the trailer was open, out I walked. I knew I was matted, with long dirty hair. Oh, how I wished they could have seen me in my prime and at my best, but I still had pride and lifted my head high. But, there was no worry, something happened the second I met her gaze. In an instant I could sense she was my human and she needed me. She was small, thin, and had a worried look on her face. When her eyes met mine, I knew this was home and I had found my purpose.

Into the pasture with Blondie I went. Blondie was to be my companion, but Terri was to be my fate. I would raise my head, shake my thick mane and trot over to her anytime she called my name. She would spend hours brushing and cleaning me. While she did that, she talked about family, work and problems she faced. I would lean into her and listen knowing this was a healing time for us both.

She would take me out of the pasture and I would walk and wonder around the yard. Terri always stayed with me and I felt like she absorbed some of my hurt and could feel some of the bad times I had encountered before stepping out of that big trailer in her driveway. It became a relaxing pastime for us both. When we were together, we could feel each other's spirit.

I recognized her car when she pulled in the driveway, usually on her way home from work. I would trot up to the gate and she would stop to spend a few minutes with me before going up to the house. These calming moments were some of the best of my life. I would shake my head to scold her for leaving me to go to work and she would laugh and tell me I was the horse of her dreams and I was her true love.

One cold day in February I became ill. I had felt my age creeping up on me for several years. My life would have been much shorter if I had not come here to live. I was loved, nourished and treated so well that it prolonged my life. It was my time to go and my only regret was my human buddy was left to mourn. My last thoughts were of our special times together. I closed my eyes and I could see myself trotting toward her and shaking my head.

ALL THINGS GOOD

I visited his grave with a small bouquet of bright yellow daffodils. As I knelt down to place them on the little mound of grass it took me back to when Tank first came into our lives.

It was late summer, and Jock and I had talked about getting a companion for our horse, Blondie, but hadn't yet decided on anything. A friend who had been coming out on a weekly basis to help train Blondie mentioned that she knew a couple who were trying to re-home an older miniature horse. The couple had large horses that bullied him around when they fed, and he kept escaping the fence.

So, on a whim, Jock said, "Bring him out and we will take him." The next day a big Chevy truck with a stock trailer pulled in the driveway. It opened up and out walked Tank. He was maybe thirty-two inches high with matted, dirty long hair. You could tell he had been neglected. My first thought was they could have brought Tank out in a van. He seemed pitiful and looked more like a goat then a miniature horse. I was worried that he might not do well with us and Blondie. But something happened the second Tank looked at me. An instant connection seemed to pass between us.

Into the pasture with Blondie he went with no hesitation. He seemed to adjust well to his new home. When I would call his name, Tank would raise his head, shake his thick mane and trot over to me. I would take him out of the pasture and spend hours brushing and cleaning him. I loved turning him loose and walking with him as he wondered around the yard. It became a relaxing pastime for us both. When we were together worry, stress and anxiety would disappear. Both human and horse could just live in the moment and enjoy our time together.

Tank recognized my car when it pulled in the driveway, usually on my way home from work. He would come trotting up to the gate and I would stop to spend a few minutes with him before going up to the house. Tank came to represent all the best things in my life. He was gentle, sweet, and there was no meanness in him, just pure loving goodness that touched my heart. I cherished those moments and looked forward to them every day.

One cold day in February Jock came to the house from feeding and told me Tank was not doing well. The veterinarian came out but offered little hope of Tank recovering. Jock spent three nights in the barn soothing and caring for Tank. But Tank was very old and it was just his time. He would not survive, and we lost our little buddy.

Tank was buried under a little tree overlooking the pasture. Jock fashioned a homemade grave marker that simply says Tank on it. Sometimes, in the quiet mornings before the alarm goes off, in the time between sleep and wakefulness, I see Tank in my mind trotting toward me and shaking his head. I relive our special time together and take a moment to think of all things good. Tank lives on in spirit and in my heart.

A COWBOY'S WISDOM

A cowboy's wisdom is whispered throughout the hills and valleys. He is independent and true, solid like the oak.

A nod and handshake is his word. He is at peace with himself and owes no explanations. His hands are calloused and weathered, but tender, as he helps a newborn foal come into the world.

His home is the open land. He begins his day by feeding and tending his horses' needs first. They have a mutual respect for each other. There is a spiritual connection between them as they trust each other while riding through dangerous terrain. Each one knowing the other will forge through with caution and grace. At the end of a long hard day's work, he still sits tall upon his saddle, knowing he has done his best.

A CONTENTED LIFE

Sunrise would find him putting on his shoes and brewing a pot of coffee. He slips on his favorite faded jacket, puts an apple in his pocket, and steps out the backdoor. With coffee in hand, he walks down the grassy lane to the fence as the horse trots up to the gate. She knickers and nuzzles his shoulder as he pets her soft nose, then gives her the apple. On he walks and checks on the cows and looks out over the land he farmed for many years, now passed down to his children. He felt contented with his life. Next, he walks down the grassy lane to a little woodshop, where there he spends his time building wooden crosses. He glues them to a wood base that holds a small white Bible. On the front of the base he writes the words "He is Risen." His family and friends give these to people throughout the area. I have one and I cherish it.

A contented life.

Mac, Sugar, Ginny

Positive Words
Positive People
Positive Life

PICNIC WITH A SQUIRREL

I was taking a little break from work
I walked to a quiet secluded place
I took some snacks and a book
Ready to enjoy a slower pace

A gray squirrel approached me
And cocked his little head
I was really quite surprised
When he sat close by, pointed to my lunch and said

Are you going to eat that apple?
Maybe you will share it some with me
I've been scurrying about all day
I'm hungry as can be
So I shared my lunch with the squirrel...

As he told me about creatures that lived near
He said the mice steal from him
But he really liked the deer

He told me chipmunks talk too much
And wild turkey can be rude
They never speak when they walk by
Momma hen and her brood

He said the fox was sneaky
And snakes will tell a lie
Raccoons will stop and visit awhile
And rabbits are terribly shy

I've tried to find that secluded spot again
I knew I was a lucky girl
To spend some time in that magical place
And picnic with a squirrel

MIRACLES HAPPEN

She sat cross-legged on the ground
Confusion and questions filled her mind
Growing up and facing the world
Is scary sometimes

Overwhelmed by life's problems
She felt so alone
Her family would be worried
She ran away from home

She looked up to the Heavens
And prayed one more time
She said, "Dear Lord, help me,
Give me a sign."

A gentle breeze touched her
A peace filled her soul
A voice from our Lord
Said, "I want you to know, miracles
Happen every now and then.
Sometimes the way is hard.
You have to understand, nothing in the
World is worth running from your life.
Just follow in mercy's path, find the
Answers by and by."

Don't be discouraged
Just keep pressing on
Be a light in the darkness that
Shines for everyone

FALL FOR NITA

The hummingbirds are gone now
There's a coolness in the air
The leaves are changing colors
Some trees are almost bare

The days are much shorter
The nights are crisp and clear
The moon and stars shine so bright
You can tell that Fall is here

God's beauty is abundant
This special time of year
Blessings unfold around us
His presence is so near

Let's not take our lives for granted
Let's be thankful everyday
Tomorrow comes way too soon
And this time shall pass away

I wrote this poem after my best friend, Nita Mace, died. She and her husband Jim used to come up every Fall from South Carolina and sit on the porch. She was Jock's cousin. I would give anything to sit on the porch with her again and watch the hummingbirds.

REFLECTION

Always on the outside
Forever looking in
Thinking of what I should have done
And where I could have been

Wondering where the years have gone
Scared of what lies ahead
Wanting to find a contented place
But my mind is full of dread

Needing to right the wrongs of life
As I walk my memory's road
Learning it's about compassion
Forgiving and letting go

THE WOMAN

In rememberance of
Iva H. Ridenour
July 5, 1916 -
January 19, 2008

Who is that woman
Staring back at me
I think I've seen her before
Take me closer, let me see

She looks so familiar
I know I've seen her some place
Let's get a little closer
I want to see her face

Her hazel eyes are similar
To someone long ago
But her hair wasn't gray then
Who is that woman, I just don't know

It was her reflection
She was seeing in a mirror
Years had stolen her memory
Her thinking wasn't clear

Who is that woman?

My eyes see,

My ears hear,

My memory fades,

But, my walk is sometimes slow,

It's me inside,

Please don't let go.

- *Anonymous*

MY SONG

No one to talk to
No place to turn
The world keeps moving
No one's concerned

Take a look deep in my eyes
Can you see my pain?
Do you understand why?

Take a look deep in my eyes
See my pain
Help me know why

I hurt so bad
Sometimes I'm numb
I just want to laugh
I want to have fun

The sunshine comes in
Happy voices fill the air
Family surrounds with blessings
And relieves my despair

I feel truly blessed to have come from such a wonderful family. I am thankful for Jock, my animals, and my art. They light up my life and complete me. I am happy..

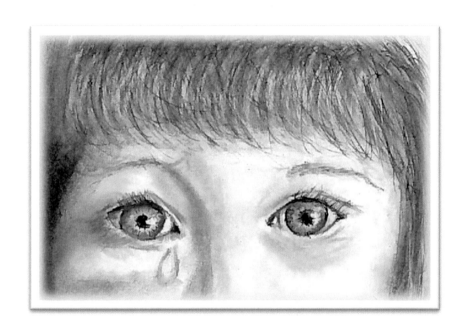

A great man is he who does not lose his child's heart.
-   *Mencius*

A CULTURED GIRL'S WORLD

A cultured girl loves adventure and travels
She is inquisitive about the world around her

She enjoys nature and studies the animals
She realizes that although there are struggles in life

Hard work and patience reap rewards
She is bright, confident and happy

Moving ever forward
Her strength is empowering

THE CHILD INSIDE

She closed her tired weathered eyes and relaxed her tense weary body. Slowly her mind wondered back through the years, giving way to a simpler time and place. She saw her, knew her, felt a presence; it was the child inside.

The child was wading in a creek bed. This was her special place where she spent hours at play. Her pant legs were rolled up to her knees and the cool water felt refreshing on her hot, dusty feet. She carried a silver bucket in her hands and was trying to catch the minnows that were swimming about. A pretty rock caught her eye and she held it up to the sunshine to inspect it closer. It was a shimmering pearly white stone. She stuck it in her pocket along with the others. It was late afternoon and shadows cast about from the tall trees. As the evening twilight lingered, it took on a spooky quality Dropping the bucket hastily, she crammed her chubby feet into a tattered pair of canvas shoes and ran as fast as her pudgy legs would go. The hair on the back of her neck stood up. Out of the woods and dark shadows she ran. She didn't slow down until she saw the lights of home in the distance. Only then did she look back and feel safe that nothing was following her. She made her way to the house where she joined the rest of the family and some neighbors gathered on the front porch. They were telling stories and laughing. Her father was playing a harmonica as her middle brother, Ron, played along softly on a guitar, while her mother and grandmother sang. They were old, familiar songs that she had heard many times before and they were soothing to the child.

She joined some of the neighbor children in the yard catching lightening bugs and playing hide and seek. The night was clear and crisp, with stars shining brightly and a silvery full moon so light that it felt like she could reach up and pick it out of the sky. A whippoorwill called in the distance. As the night rolled on, the neighbors bid their goodbyes and strolled off into the darkness. The child sat in a big overstuffed rocking chair as the rest of the family ambled into the house. Sleepy, and filled with childhood contentment she thought those days would go on forever. Startled and scared, her eyes opened as she glanced around the room in confusion. Slowly, she realized she was in a bed in a long-term care nursing facility. Laying back, she once again closed her eyes and waited for the child inside to return to her with a new adventure.

WINTER'S EDGE

Winter's blanket of snow shimmers
Underneath a moonlit sky
Snowflakes fall silently
As a herd of deer pass by

Hot chocolate is steaming on the stove as
I add another log to the fire
I read and relax
The crackling flames dance
I yawn, it's time to retire

The holidays pass shared with family
And friends, new memories made
But the cold never ends

The icy winds blow
Boredom has me pacing the floors
Cabin fever sets in
I want sunshine when I
Look out my doors

Finally, I see a robin
Perched upon a hedge
I smile and relax
It helps to relieve
The cold winter's edge

A ROUND HOUSE

I want to live in a round house
Not a square one that has dark corners and gloom.

I want to live where there is music
And happy people, where there is no such thing as nightmares or fear.

I want to be where warmth and love surround me.
I want to live in a round house.

Donald and Terri

Calmness abides

Darkness ebbs

The circle rolls

Our home place

Grandma

Grandma's cottage

Front, left to right: Jesse, Mary, and Ronald
Back: Terri, Diana (Dee), and Donald

Lawrence (Don) Mash
Mattie Bright Mash
Our Parents

WHEN KINDNESS GOES AWAY

Let's not be too judgmental
About our neighbors
Or be quick to criticize our friends
I have done these things before
And it never had a good end

My neighbor brought my runaway horse back
My friends brought food when I was ill
I felt bad about my ugly words
And do to this day still

Gossip and rumors can be so hurtful
Let's be careful what we say
Mean words linger too long
When kindness goes away

Be kind to each other always.

Mighty oaks

from

little acorns

grow.

IN LOVING MEMORY OF MATTIE MASH ON MOTHER'S DAY
By Mary McKnight Whalen

Mom, you taught us right from wrong and honesty is always best.
You punished us many times when we put you to the test.

You sacrificed things for us from the time we were very small.
When we let you down, you loved us through it all.

You taught us to stand together as a family and we do.
There's only one thing missing now Mom, and that is you.
We love and miss you.

Jesse, Mary, Ronald, Diana, Donald, Terri

114

A Cultured Girl

Terri Mash
Writer and Illustrator

About the Author

Terri was born to Lawrence and Mattie Mash, the youngest of six children. Raised in Ohio, with a love of art and music engrained in her soul, she would doodle, draw, and write song lyrics then stash them in a closet. It wasn't until recently she got the courage to pursue her passions. Self-taught with a relentless spirit, Terri fulfilled her dream.

Made in the USA
Middletown, DE
01 July 2021